A Whizz Along The Wall

By DENIS INCH

Illustrated by PAUL TAYLOR

WHOOSH! BOOKS

First published 2000 by
Whoosh! Books,
1 Bank Hall,
Hallbankgate,
Brampton,
Cumbria,
CA8 2NP

ISBN 0 9538252 0 5

Printed in Great Britain by
Unicorn,
Brampton,
Cumbria,
CA8 1TR.
www.unicornqpg.co.uk

What you're in for!

Acknowledgements

I am indebted to a large number of scholars who have written on the subjects of Hadrian's Wall, the Romans in Britain and the ancient Romans in general. Some of their works are listed at the end of this book.
I also gratefully acknowledge generous support and help at various stages of preparing this publication from Nick Winterbotham, Tony Wilmott, Nils Minor and Eileen Norman. However, responsibility for any shortcomings it may contain rests with me.
Denis Inch

Just for starters!

HADRIAN'S Wall appeals to the imagination.

It once marked the lonely frontier on the far northern limit of a great empire. It straddled a misty, little-known island beyond the great ocean which bounded the ancient world.

Its essential idea was both simple and grand — a big barrier flung straight across the land from one sea to the other.

It draws visitors not only from all over Britain but from all over the world, particularly from the United States, Japan, Germany, the Netherlands and Belgium — and also from Italy, whose citizens sometimes feel that in a way the Wall is theirs at least as much as ours.

Many visitors take in the Wall en route from Newcastle or York to Edinburgh. Perhaps they have only a few hours to spare to look at a monument on which they could easily spend a long weekend, if not a week — or even a lifetime.

This little book is for them. There are excellent publications which explain in detail the fascinating story of Hadrian's Wall (and we don't know it all yet!), but this is meant to be an easy approach to a complex subject.

It's a taster, an hors-d'oeuvre, an easily digestible morsel to get the juices flowing before sticking your teeth into bigger and meatier books.

Bon appetit!

Welcome words on the Wall

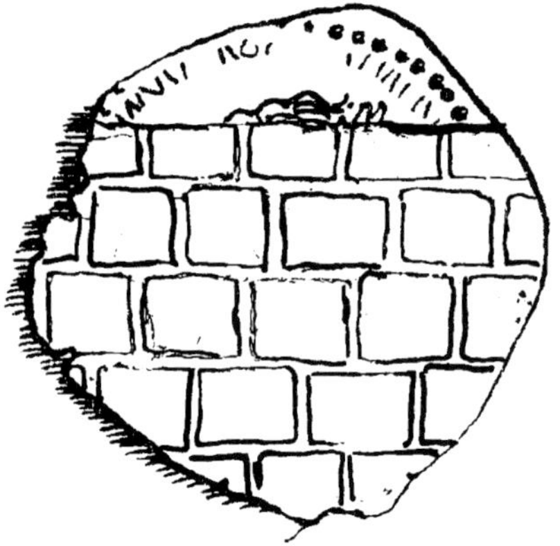

THE Roman world had seen nothing quite like it before. . . a fortified wall running straight for mile after mile from coast to coast, studded with strongholds big and small.

It was an engineering extravaganza and it cost a bomb.

But one emperor was prepared to abandon it not long after another had built it.

And it's still here! And it's the top Roman monument north of the Alps! Now it's a World Heritage Site, ranking with the Taj Mahal in India and the Great Wall of China.

But about 1,400 years ago its builders said: "We're off — you're welcome to it ."

So, welcome to the Wall.

And welcome to these words about what it was, when it was, how it was, why it was, what's become of it and the who's who of the Wall.

We'll start with the bloke who had the bright idea in the first place, Hadrian.

Hairy happy Hadrian!

OUR man Publius Aelius Hadrianus was born in sunny Spain and was adopted by his relative, the Emperor Trajan. Before Trajan popped off in 117AD, he nominated Hadrian to take over the top job.

As emperors go, Hadrian was a nice guy. He gave loadsa dosh to the poor, was kind to slaves, loved his wife as well as his boyfriend, and was a matey sort of bloke, ready with a quip when you bumped into him in the public baths.

He liked building, in the sense of watching grand edifices rise up at his command, but naturally he stood aside to let someone else heave the hod and mix the mortar.

He built a very des. res. at Tivoli in the foothills outside Rome, as well as the Pantheon dedicated to all the city's gods, and new towns all over the place. And, most famously, he built Hadrian's Wall.

He was also famous in his day for growing a beard, so setting a new style for facial hair. After suffering for centuries under the tyranny of the Greek fashion for a naked chin, Roman men were freed from the agony of the barber's iron razor, tweezers and disgusting depilatory goo of bat's blood and donkey fat.

Hadrian was also in his forties. In fact, he was nothing at all like the limp, beardless youth whose image stands on

a plinth above his name in the Roman wall town of Brampton.

Trajan had carried on the longstanding tradition of tacking substantial new bits onto the empire, particularly in and around Dacia, now known as Romania. He let the world know all about it in a cartoon strip carved on a column which still stands in Rome. Hadrian broke with this tradition, too.

The empire was at its peak and he decided it was time to stop going for growth and settle for what he'd got. A man who knew where to draw the line, Hadrian set off on a tour of the property to do just that.

On the continent he fixed several boundaries, mostly using natural features like rivers and the sea. Then he came to Britain, the first emperor to cross the Channel since Claudius trailed in glory after his conquering army about 80 years earlier.

When Hadrian got to Britain in 122AD it seems there was some sort of riot going on in the north. After sorting that out, he decided it was pointless to keep battering the Caledonians just for the sake of owning all that Highland scenery. He drew another line from the River Tyne in the east (modern Newcastle, the land of the Geordies) to the Solway Firth (west of modern Carlisle, encroaching on the land of the marras*) and said: "Build a wall."

And that's how Britain got another World Heritage Site. We already had Stonehenge, of course.

* *See footnote, page 30.*

Well! What a Wall!

BUILD a wall, eh? There's more to Hadrian's Wall than just a wall.

Nobody gets to be masters of the world by using carpet tacks where two six-inch nails will do — and the Romans always did a proper job. The Wall was just one of several features of a military zone which ran east-west from Tyne to Solway.

There was no chance of blundering through it unawares in the dark while out rustling your neighbour's shorthorns. And if you wanted to cross on legit business, you had to ask nicely.

It's a good idea to spend a few minutes getting the plan of it in your head. It helps you see the picture better when looking at the remaining masonry and the bumps in the ground. This is the way a member of the Brigantes tribe who lived south of the Wall, travelling to visit his cousins in the north, would see what the Romans had done:

• First, the big earthwork known as the vallum. Now "vallum" sounds like it should mean "wall" but not here, it doesn't — it's a big ditch (Confused? Page 20 will sort you out.) Whether it went through soft clay or hard rock, it was always 20ft wide at the top with sloping sides, and 10ft deep with a flat bottom. The diggers tipped the soil clear of the ditch to make continuous mounds on each side. The vallum runs south of the Wall along its whole length.

• Secondly, a paved road 20ft wide, soldiers, for the marching of, along the Wall. Built some time later, it is known as the Military Way, not to be confused with the Military Road, the modern B6318 we post-Romans motor along to reach the Wall today (we'll come to the Military Road later). The Military Way went from milecastle to milecastle.

• Thirdly, the Wall itself, a daunting 15-20ft high, stretching as far away as you could see. Along it at every Roman mile (a bit shorter than ours) was a miniature fort with its own garrison guarding a gateway. In between each of these milecastles were two smaller turrets, just for keeping an eye on things.

• Fourthly, north of the wall there was the standard Roman army defensive ditch, about 25-30ft wide and up to 11ft deep. This was to slow down any belligerent barbarians. The soil dug out was spread out low on the far side so that cunning Caledonians couldn't creep up unseen behind it.

• Fifthly, every six or seven miles (11km) along the wall you would meet one of a dozen full-size forts. These were built for the soldiers who kept an eye on the whole system. The forts came out of the army manual, built to

the same rectangular plan all over the world. Whether he'd been out on Greek retsina or British beer, a legionary could lurch his way back to the right barracks at night.

There'd not been anything quite like it in the Roman world. Ditches were routine; soldiers dug them in their sleep. Fortlets strung out over dodgy bandit country; yep, done that. But nobody had joined up the dots before with an actual wall. Hadrian had scored a first.

But why a wall? What was the big idea? Hadrian's Wall wasn't a defence. Roman soldiers didn't generally like defending walls and forts — they liked to get out in the fresh air, bash the other bloke's nose with a big shield and, while his eyes were watering, stick a short, hefty sword in his breakfast.

There's only one line about the Wall in all the ancient writings. Hadrian's biographer said: "He was the first to build a wall, 80 miles long, to separate the Romans from the barbarians." That answer poses a few questions, but all those gates in the milecastles give a clue. The tribesmen could go through, but only under the noses of the military and the customs men. It was for control. Hadrian's Wall was like a collar on the neck of Britain.

Heel, boy!

Workers on the Wall

NO ONE'S ever accused the Romans of being nice.

They liked to proceed in straight lines and anyone in the way got a hobnailed sandal up their seat. The line of the Wall, as unbending as possible, ploughed straight across farmers' furrows, wiped out at least one hamlet and probably divided local families.

It stuck to the high ground, so that in Northumberland it clings to the crest of the geological feature formed by the Whin Sill, which resembles a huge petrified wave in the landscape, with loughs shining at the feet of its steep crags. In Cumbria the Wall runs along the heights overlooking the River Irthing.

It's lovely country and a dramatic setting. What did the Romans ever do for us? Ask the tourist board and the bed and breakfast ladies.

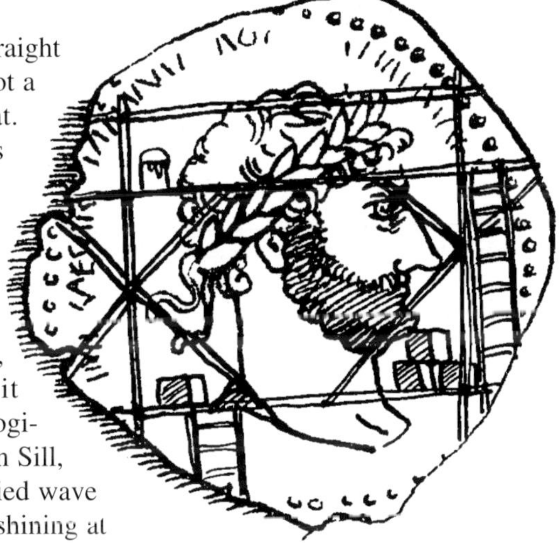

Hadrian swanned off to do business elsewhere and left the legions to get on with it.

They had surveyors and engineers, smiths, masons and carpenters — everything they needed except JCBs. Working west from Pons Aelius, which is modern Newcastle, some squads built milecastles and turrets while others followed along filling in with the Wall.

The original plan was too neat to be true, with a nice little milecastle at exactly every mile and turrets at regulation distance — just the kind of thing the legionaries might expect from some headquarters desk-jockey who'd never got his boots muddy.

On the real, humpy-bumpy ground, with the right materials not always available, and with the locals looking surly about the whole idea, somebody had to adapt the blueprint to reality.

So, as soon as the squaddies got stuck into the stonemasonry, the generals started mucking them about. "Just take everything along a bit further east to Wallsend, will you, chaps? . . . Tell you what, let's build some forts right up on the Wall, shall we? . . . Dig this vallum for us as well, if you wouldn't mind . . . Well, what I'm saying is that we don't need to make this Wall so wide, OK? . . . When you get west of the River Irthing, don't use stone, use turf . . . No, no, listen, I'm telling you, we're using stone all the way . . . Y'know, we ought to have a proper road to link up these milecastles . . ."

No wonder one soldier called Daminius scratched his name at a stone quarry and added: "I didn't want to do it." Anyone who's worked for any large organisation, whether it's a supermarket chain or the Roman Army, knows how he felt.

By the way, the orders were indeed to build a wall of turf west of the Irthing, but it wasn't long before a stone wall was built on top.

But after eight years or so, there it was — Hadrian's Wall.

Then, 16 years after he ordered the Wall, Hadrian died. The new emperor, Antoninus Pius, was a new broom — and Antoninus swept north.

It was "Forward march" into Caledonia, and a new wall — the Antonine Wall — was built of turf 100 miles farther up-country between the Firth of Forth and the River Clyde.

Hadrian's Wall was largely abandoned. Doors were taken off milecastles and anyone and their auntie wandered through at will. The old barrier began to crumble.

Veterans in the army, whinging about the wasted effort, would doubtless remember how they'd sweated over those stones. But after a while the generals did a U-turn and decided Hadrian's Wall was the best boundary after all ("Y'mean we sweated blood over that Antonine Wall fer nowt, fer absobloodylutely nowt?")

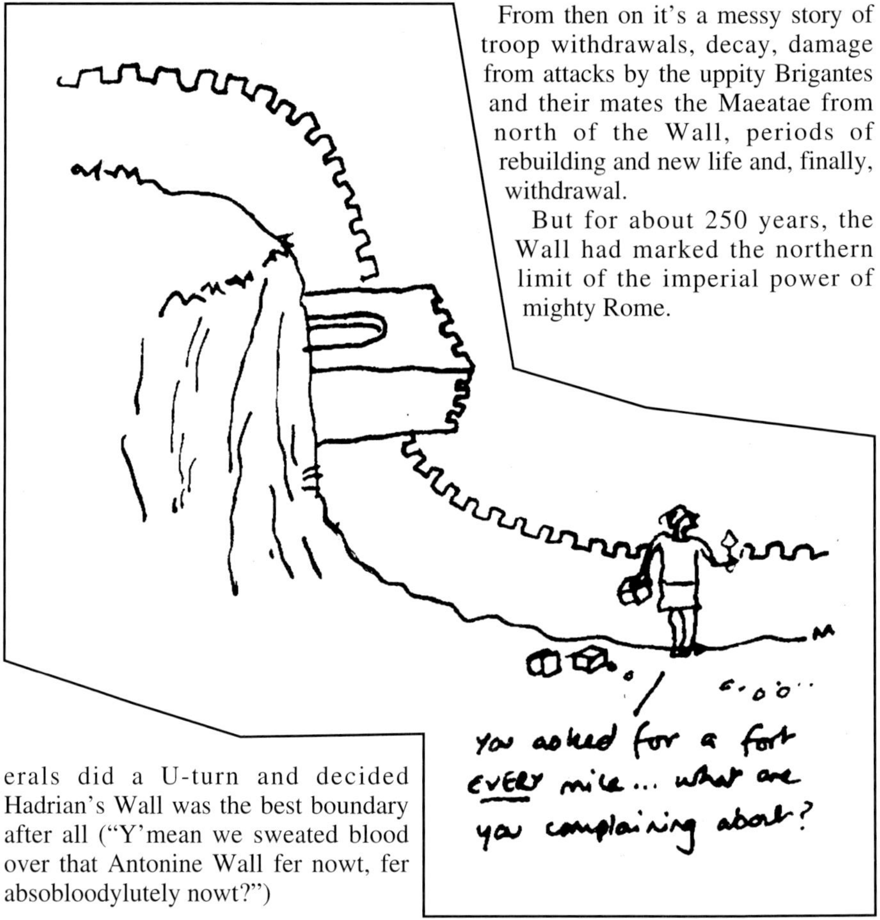

From then on it's a messy story of troop withdrawals, decay, damage from attacks by the uppity Brigantes and their mates the Maeatae from north of the Wall, periods of rebuilding and new life and, finally, withdrawal.

But for about 250 years, the Wall had marked the northern limit of the imperial power of mighty Rome.

Home, home on the Wall

THERE'S a poetic image of lice-ridden, shivering Italian soldiers patrolling the wall, cursing their billet in dark, misty, rain-soaked, windswept, benighted northern Britain, longing for the olive groves of home beside a shimmering, blue Mediterranean, and pining for Mama's pasta and the girl they left behind them.

Mmmm, not quite spot on. The sun does shine sometimes in Cumbria and Northumberland and the long, light summer evenings allowed plenty of time to get to know the friendly local midges — and no doubt the local lasses, too. Besides, the lads of the legions, although citizens of Rome, came from all over the empire and might have known worse weather at home. In any case, after building the Wall, the skilled and elite legionaries went back to barracks for a hot bath and to get new orders. It was left to the auxiliary units to man the newfangled barrier.

Like the legions, the auxiliary regiments were a polyglot lot. In just about every spot ruled from Rome worried, tearful mums had waved goodbye as their boys joined up to see the world. Soldiering for Rome was a job for life (even if it might be a short one) with the reward of Roman citizenship for the tribesman volunteer at the end of a 25-year stint.

So there were Lingonians from eastern France and Nervians from Belgium stationed at Wallsend; Newcastle was garrisoned by our very own Cornovians from the English-Welsh border country, as well as Vangians from the Upper Rhineland; Hungarian Pannonians were on duty at Halton Chesters; Batavians from Holland at Carrawburgh; Tungrians, another Belgian tribe, at Housesteads and Castlesteads, Bavarian and Swiss mountaineers of the Raetian tribe at Great Chesters; Dalmatians from the eastern Adriatic and Hanians from Syria at Carvoran; Bulgarian Thracians and Romanian Dacians at Birdoswald; Gauls from France at Castlesteads and Stanwix; Mauretanians from North Africa and Rhineland Germans at Burgh by Sands. Asturians from north-west Spain were to be found in many a barrack room in the wall area, including South Shields, Newcastle, Chesters and Great

Chesters. Also stationed in the fort at South Shields were boatmen who had learned their trade on the River Tigris in Syria.

But as time went on it was local lads who were recruited to fill the gaps in units named for faraway places, and perhaps few of them had ever seen an olive grove. As for home cooking, many soldiers tasted it every night in the little towns which grew up outside the fort walls. That's where their wives — both official and unofficial — lived. And perhaps after dinner the boys who were far from home forgot all about the girls they'd left behind them.

For much of its two-and-a-half centuries as a frontier, the Wall offered a peaceful life. Soldiers wrote home asking for socks. Officers' wives organised birthday parties. Racist NCOs sneered and sniggered at the "little Britties".

But nothing lasts for ever. The Romans didn't march out of Britain the way Britain beat a ceremonial retreat from India and Hong Kong. They sort of drifted away. Nothing personal, but they were busy with big problems nearer home.

The burghers of the Romano-British towns finally got the message in

410AD. They asked the emperor to help them see off Germanic raiders. The answer was: "Sorry, gents, you'll have to sort it out yourselves." The Romans had gone: No more pay parades for the squaddies — but no more imperial tax demands for the locals, either.

So the British lads who had been manning the wall probably pointed out, in the nicest possible way, of course, that, having been trained in best practice with leading players in the global security industry, they fortunately found themselves able to offer best value in community defence and law enforcement, etc, etc.

In the local hovels, it probably looked like an offer you couldn't refuse. The peasants paid up.

And at Birdoswald the new bosses built a big timber hall, where they celebrated the coming of the Dark Ages with beer and beef.

The Wall's downfall had begun.

Daylight robbery!

THE present state of the Wall may arouse suspicion that someone's backed a wagon up and hauled it away.

Too right! In the bad old days the heritage industry used to be all about recycling. Medieval farmers would turn up with an ox-cart and a few strong lads and lug the Wall away by the ton. Wouldn't you if you had a barn, a stone dyke, or a farmhouse to build next door?

And if you'd ruined your ploughshares on the remains of a milecastle, you'd send the lads up again just to get the cussed foundations out of the blessed way, wouldn't you?

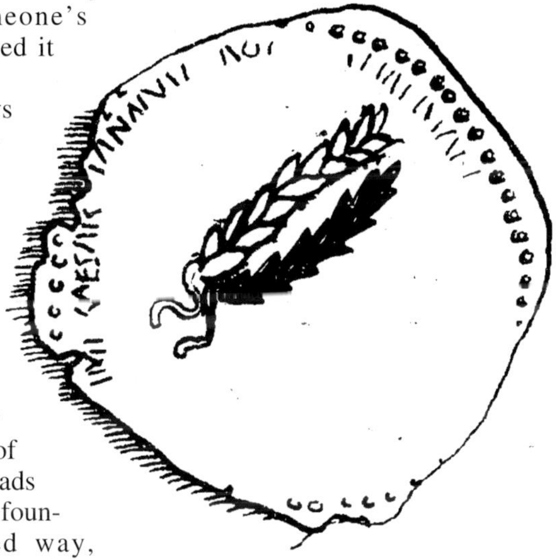

It has been known for there to be an embarrassment of Roman stone in the area even in modern times. I was once offered a few loads at the end of an archaeological dig. Sadly, at the time I couldn't afford the haulage costs.

But not so long ago a local builder made a bungalow home out of Roman stone. Pull into the car park of the Milecastle Inn near Cawfields and read the plaque in front of the little bungalow of Burnstead. It tells passers-by how it was built in 1970 by Mr Albert Burns of Bardon Mill, using surplus stone from an excavation at Housesteads fort.

After so much daylight robbery in centuries past there's perhaps as much Wall to be seen off the Wall as on it. The farmhouse at Sewingshields, sitting on top of a turret site, is built out of Roman stone and it's not the only one.

Two hundred years ago an old antiquarian tearfully pleaded with a farmer not to take any more of the 200 yard stretch he was wheeling away for a new house at Brunton Bank above the North Tyne. Some of the biggest filchers were priors and prelates wanting to put up churches — see Lanercost Priory.

Not only building stone went missing but other bits and pieces like the small altars with which the legionaries paid their respects to the emperor, Jupiter and other gods they collected on their travels.

Some altars have ended up as a feature in farmhouse or garden walls. Tullie House Museum in Carlisle has one that was converted into a sundial.

Another has been prised out of Carlisle Castle, where it was on duty as a door lintel.

One stone dedicated to pagan Jupiter was converted to serve another religion in the choir of Lanercost Priory.

An inscription stone was taken from Vindolanda fort and over the Tyne to be recycled as a tombstone in Beltingham churchyard.

After Bonnie Prince Charlie's little adventure south of the Border in 1745, the English Army found they didn't have a decent road to hop quickly across to Carlisle from Newcastle.

In the way that armies do, they liberated a whole lot more of their Roman colleagues' work, especially from Carrawburgh fort.

They used it to build the Military Road, the B6318, which runs on top of the Wall's foundations for miles west of Newcastle, despite the protests of antiquary William Stukeley.

More recently, much of the wall has vanished under the sprawling streets and factories of Tyneside and in quarries at places like Cawfields.

Unsophisticated Bedouin tribesmen are reported to have used Dead Sea scrolls for firelighters before smarter desert dwellers found that collectors paid cash for them. How much of the past has been destroyed almost under our noses?

Some is saved only by chance, like the choice pieces of masonry which vanished down south in the 18th century and nearly didn't make it back.

They had been collected by a recorder of Carlisle, William Gilpin, at his home at Scaleby Castle, just outside the city.

Somehow they came to be sold to another gent with antique tastes, who thought they would add a romantic touch to the makeover of his garden in Surrey in 1758.

In 1923 an architect saw a fancy pig trough in a Surrey farmyard was about to be broken up for builder's rubble.

He saved the altar, alerted a noted archaeologist of the day, and the stones were rounded up and brought safely back to home territory at Tullie House Museum in Carlisle.

What other little treasures have not been saved and have crumbled under the workman's hammer?

We'll never know.

Who's who on the Wall

YOU'RE not the first, you know! There was a whole busload of people last week!

In fact, there's been a growing stream of tourists and antiquaries peering over the Wall over the last 400 years.

Scholars have scratched their greying heads and seriously asked: "What does it all mean?"

Some have been heroes in the fight to save it. Others, including the creator of Wicked Wanda, have brought it all to life for the newcomers.

Earliest visitor to write about the Wall was the Venerable Bede, eighth-century monk and historian, who popped over from Jarrow, just across the River Tyne from Wallsend.

Then it was fairly quiet until Elizabethan times, when antiquarian studies became trendy.

William Camden, headmaster of Westminster School, visited most of the Wall on foot for his guide book to Britain in 1599. True to type, the perambulatory pedagogue wrote it up in Latin. He'd given the best bit — the central section — a miss for fear of "rank robbers". You see, it was poor

country and farmers roundabouts practised diversification long before you could get grants for it, mostly by way of lifting other people's livestock and unsecured chattels.

Camden's conclusion that the vallum was built by Hadrian and the wall by Severus, who was emperor two generations later, from AD 193 to 211, was accepted for 250 years.

Then a passionate pilgrim strode onto the scene. William Hutton, a Birmingham businessman, set out on foot at the age of 78 in 1801, walked through the Lakes to Carlisle, marched twice along the length of the wall and back home, clocking up 601 miles in 35 days.

Local folk didn't know what to make of him and took him at various times for a clergyman, a government spy, a Methodist preacher, or a surveyor for taxes or land enclosure.

It was Hutton who, with tears in his eyes, begged a farmer not to pull down any more Wall to build a new house at Brunton Bank and did manage to save a few particularly interesting yards, which are still there. In less than a year he had published an enthusiastic history of the monument.

A clergyman, the Rev John Skinner, who walked along the wall the same

REV. SKINNER APPEALS TO THE NATIVES

year as Hutton, complained sniffily to his diary: "Civility to strangers by no means appears to be a characteristic of the country people of Northumberland."

Even their dogs had an attitude problem, he found. But perhaps Skinner was the one with the problem, writing sentences like that.

A lot of walkers have gone over the Wall since then, however, and a lady writer in the 1920s, Jessie Mothersole, had a different experience.

Sheltering from a thunderstorm in a farmhouse, she was given cheese, jam, scones, white and brown bread and two kinds of cake. "Sorry I've nowt fer tea," said the farmer's wife, and refused Jessie's money.

The hospitality of modern innkeepers and farm B&B wives around Heddon, Hexham and Haltwhistle is now attested by strangers from all over the globe.

Camden's error was put right in 1839 by the Rev John Hodgson, who was vicar of Bede's old patch in Jarrow.

He studied the writing on the Wall left by the lads who built it. The carved inscriptions, which are couched in abbreviations like a modern estate agent's small ad, told which army unit worked on which section and showed that the Wall was definitely built by Hadrian, not Severus.

Hero of the Wall was John Clayton (1792-1890), lawyer, famous town clerk of Newcastle and scholar.

Clayton owned the estate which included the fort of Chesters, which he explored, along with surrounding forts, milecastles and turrets. He bought land to save stretches of Wall and probably holds a record for owning five Roman forts, including Housesteads, Chesters and Vindolanda.

The handy-sized book that intense and serious-looking visitors pull out on arriving at each fort or turret is likely to be an edition of John Collingwood Bruce's Handbook To The Roman Wall.

Northumberland-born Bruce, a Newcastle headmaster, became a leading authority on the Wall and in 1863 he published a short guide which, revised and extended, is still the one for walkers' rucksacks.

In 1849 Bruce organised the first "pilgrimage" along the Wall to show his rather disbelieving fellow-historians and their ladies its treasures. Less of a picnic than they used to be, the "pilgrimages" for Wall scholars are now held every ten years and the twelfth took place in August 1999.

One bloke asking another bloke he'd just met in a Moroccan hotel to draw him a picture of other blokes sitting on the loo sounds like extreme social recklessness. However, it was the start of a highly successful publishing partnership which never once looked like getting bogged down.

The artist was the late Ronald Embleton, whose image of soldiers using the latrine at Housesteads fort became a postcard bestseller. Embleton, who had previously paid the bills by doing everything from children's books to drawing drawers-less Wanda for a men's magazine, was the illustrator Frank Graham had been looking for.

Together, Graham, a Newcastle historian and publisher who had already written books about the Romans, and Embleton take the credit for bringing the Wall and its people alive for hundreds of thousands of visitors.

If you get lost despite all the brown signs, you're in good company. Kevin Costner had local cinemagoers cackling when he dressed up like Robin Hood, and it wasn't just the tights. It was because first stop on his way from Dover to Nottingham was Hadrian's Wall.

For workers on the Wall, the most frequently asked question is: "Where was that shot of K. Costner in Robin Hood, Prince Of Thieves?" Answer: "Sycamore Gap."

You can't miss it. It's a gap with a sycamore tree in it. Get the kids to look out for it as you drive along the Military Road — it'll stop them fighting in the back seat.*

Our Kev wasn't the only confused visitor. Read on.

(*Oh, all right. See page 24.)

Which Wall was that?

PAINFULLY, I picked through my little store of German words, trying to get across the idea of "Hadrian's Wall".

My friends from Münster were puzzled. At long last a light dawned in their eyes: "Ah, ja, Hadd-rianz-va-a-arll," they growled.

Why didn't I think of that? No fancy foreign words needed, just a heavy German accent.

But it's taken a while for the monument to become almost universally known as Hadrian's Wall, or the Roman Wall.

The Venerable Bede longwindedly referred to it as "the wall with which the Romans divided the island of Britain".

Bede takes the blame for a little confusion about the name of the great ditch which runs south of the Wall.

He called it the vallum, which sounds to non-Latin speakers as though it might be the name for the Wall itself — and "vallum" does mean "rampart". The Romans probably called the vallum something like "fossa" (ditch), which would be a better description, but Bede's name has stuck.

Five centuries after Bede another historian-monk, Matthew Paris, wrote about the "wall which divided the English and the Picts in times past". Oops, sorry, Matt, couple of slips there which anyone could make (and people still do).

The English hadn't appeared yet. Their ancestors — the Angles, Jutes and Saxons and so forth — were still dossing about on the continent in Hadrian's time.

They were thinking about making a nuisance of themselves with part-time piracy, but hadn't yet written into their business plan the takeover and re-branding of southern Britain.

The Picts, too, had not then been invented — the first mention of them was about 170 years after the Wall was built.

That didn't stop folks who couldn't spell talking about "the Pict Wal" , like Henry VIII's librarian, John Leland, who spent nearly a decade traipsing round Britain's antiquities in the 16th century.

In Elizabethan times Camden dropped his great brick on the Wall, saying it was all the work of the Emperor Severus. He relegated Hadrian to the role of ditch-digger, crediting him only with the vallum.

Perhaps schoolmaster Camden shouldn't be caned too hard. After all, Severus's lads had left their trademarks all over the area from ten years of rebuilding the Wall and nearby places like Corbridge and Vindolanda.

This was only about 60 or 70 years after Hadrian, and it's not clear whether the repairs were needed because of malicious vandalism by irritable local taxpayers, or because of ordinary wear and tear, or both.

By the way, Lucius Septimius Severus Pertinax was the only African to become emperor. He died at York in 211, neither the first nor the last Roman to have failed to give a final KO to the Caledonians.

Local historian Thomas Machell, writing in about 1690, said the monument had several names in several places: The Roman Wall, the Longwall, and, of course, the Picts' Wall.

Daniel Defoe, creator of Robinson Crusoe, lurking around the north on what may have been a secret police spying mission in the early 1700s, resisted looking along the famous Picts' Wall.

Curiously, he said that it had been "built by the Romans, or rather rebuilt by them". Perhaps he thought the Picts had won the original contract, or even the fairies, as some others have believed.

Talking of fairies and enchantment and such like, Sewingshields Crag is one of the innumerable places round Britain where King Arthur, Queen Guinever and their court sleep, waiting to be roused by the note of a magic horn to rule again over Britain.

Their cave was said to have been found in the late 18th century by a farmer who did everything to break the spell except blow the horn. Arthur reviled him

as a "witless wight" before sinking back into his slumber. So, except for a few lottery winners among us, that's why we're still waiting for the golden age of Camelot.

And talking of losers, the first man to order a dig at a Roman site was King John in 1201. His treasure hunt at Corbridge was in vain, however. The king's men missed the pot of gold which stayed hidden for seven centuries — a bronze jug with 160 gold coins.

More successful as plunderers were the weekend visitors to Carrawburgh after a huge cache of coins, jewellery and other offerings were found in a spring devoted to Coventina, a Celtic goddess, in 1876. More than 13,000 coins were rescued, but an unknown number vanished into trippers' pockets as souvenirs.

Unlike Coventina, Good Queen Bess kept her hand firmly on her halfpenny and much more besides.

When centuries of raiding, blackmail, rustling, murder, pillaging, burning, looting and feuding across the ill-defined English-Scottish border reached a peak in her reign, a civil servant looked to the past for a cunning plan to stop the rot.

"Got it," he told the Queen, "We could build an inskonce, like ye Picts' Wall, with rampart and ditch and a castle every mile. That would keep these troublesome northern chappies off each other's throats and wouldn't cost more than £30,000."

Always canny with cash, Elizabeth dropped his plan in the tray marked "Pending".

And so Hadrian's Wall remains unique.

Spot-on spots for Wall spotters

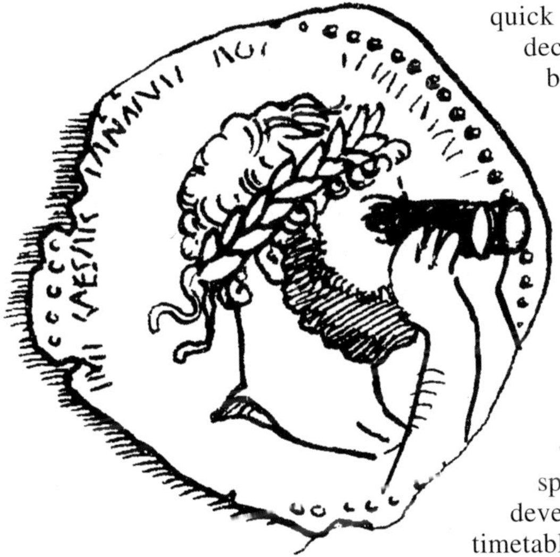

EVEN though a lot of Wall has been wheeled away, there's still lots to see — and there's usually a bit more every year as the archaeologists have another little dig each summer.

For visitors who only have time for a quick whizz round, the hard part is deciding what bits to aim for, so below there's a selection of the best sites to help plan a worthwhile visit. It should give an idea of the best spots to spot what's what on the Wall.

Haltwhistle Tourist Information Centre at Haltwhistle Station mans the hotline for the Wall (telephone 01434 322002). It keeps up to date with the latest about the Wall from end to end, including news about special events like guided walks, developments at visitor attractions, timetables for the Hadrian's Wall bus and where to meet a Roman soldier (there are quite a few knocking about at times in the summer and you might even see one on the bus).

Another useful place is the Northumberland National Park Centre at Once Brewed on the Military Road (B6318) north of Bardon Mill (open mid-March to the end of October daily 9.30am-5.30pm, telephone 01434 344777/344396).

It has lots of info about the central stretch of the Wall through the national park, including details of walks and other activities organised by park staff.

A national footpath along the Wall from Newcastle upon Tyne to Bowness-on-Solway should be fully open by 2002. Telephone the Countryside Agency (0191 232 8252) for latest info.

The Wall

The most dramatic and generally best-preserved stretch of the wall is the section between Sewingshields Crags and Greenhead.

This is where to get your boots on and march in the steps of the Romans through great scenery. Interesting strolls can also be made between Gilsland

Station and Birdoswald, taking in Poltross Burn Milecastle, Willowford Bridge over the River Irthing and Harrow Scar milecastle, perched high above the river.

The Wall hasn't survived anywhere at its full height, but the highest bit to be seen is just east of Sycamore Gap, which is east of Steel Rigg, near Twice Brewed, on the Military Road. More than 11ft high, this stretch was excavated and consolidated in the 1980s.

There is a good, if short, length remaining at Heddon-on-the-Wall, and much more between Sewingshields Crags and Walltown Crags and also between Gilsland and Birdoswald.

A reconstruction of the Wall can be seen at Vindolanda Roman Fort, where the kids can play Romans and Brigantes in the turrets.

Hadrian's legionaries ran out of limestone for mortar when they crossed over to the west of the River Irthing into sandstone country, so they started building a wall out of turf instead. In most places a stone wall was later laid along the same line, but not on a length west of Birdoswald. This is the best place to see the remains of the turf wall, with the vallum running alongside.

Milecastles

The best-preserved milecastles include the one at Poltross Burn, a short walk from the village of Gilsland. It's on such a steep slope that any rubber-legged platoon lurching back from the winebar on Saturday nights must have avalanched against the north wall.

Another worth seeing is at Winshields, near Twice Brewed, close to the highest point on the Wall.

Harrow's Scar milecastle looms high above the River Irthing. It's a pleasant trek from Birdoswald along a well-preserved bit of Wall with opportunities for a bit of phallus-spotting — see below, as they say (or see page 26).

Turrets

A good example is at Brunton, just north of the village of Wall near Hexham. The remains of several turrets can be seen on the Military Road between Birdoswald and Banks East, where there's another good one.

Vallum

Keep an eye open for the vallum beside the B6318 between East Wallhouses and Wallhouses. Look eastwards from the brow of the hill at Cawfield to see it running across the pasture. Also find it beside the road between Birdoswald and Banks west of Wall Bowers.

Defensive ditch

The ditch on the north side of the Wall is plain to see for a couple of miles beside the B6318 Military Road at Wall Houses and at Limestone Corner, where it is cut out of rock.

A NEW FASHION IS BORN

Military Way

The Roman road which Emperor Severus had built to link the milecastles can be seen between Sewingshields and Carvoran. One stretch is easily spotted running east from Cawfield, between the vallum and the Wall. It's also visible west of Limestone Corner.

Forts

Housesteads and Chesters forts are two of the best examples on the line of the Wall. Vindolanda is another interesting fort not on the Wall, but just south of it.

Off the Wall

Places built of stone robbed from the Wall include Corbridge Church; Burgh by Sands church; Thirlwall Castle near Greenhead; Chollerford Church, whose roof is held up by columns from the headquarters building at Chesters Roman fort; Lanercost Priory; the medieval castle at Bewcastle; the crypt of Hexham Abbey; Sewingshields Farm; Drumburgh Castle; Bowness Church; Stanwix Church.

Roman bridges

The remains of bridges which carried the Wall across the water are still there beside the North Tyne at Chesters, near Chollerford, and beside the River Irthing at Willowford, near Gilsland.

Other (naughty) bits

Keep your eyes open for the latrine at Housesteads Roman fort. It's become the most famous multi-hole netty in the north of England since illustrator Ronald Embleton's vision of sitting soldiers was printed on a postcard.

In the good old days there was running water, sponges on a stick instead of loo paper and plenty of company, but it's gone down the pan a bit since.

Also see if you can spot the rude good luck symbols which the soldiers carved everywhere.

In our liberated age, the censor won't stand for a merest glimpse of a phallus, but the Romans were much less rigid about these things.

They would often put them on house walls, street corners or even on jewellery (including that worn by the kids) to ward off danger and the evil eye.

At Chesters fort there is a phallus carved on the southern face of the bridge abutment; a big one on a flagstone in the courtyard of the principia,

the fort's headquarters building; and another in the lowest course of masonry in the hot room of the bath house.

There are two on the Wall between the River Irthing and Birdoswald fort. One is 211 yards west of Harrow Scar milecastle. Another is on the south side of the Wall, opposite where the road turns north beside the car park.

On this section, the presence of phalli and other carvings and inscriptions are indicated by a metal tag set into the lower courses of the stonework below.

There used to be a whopper of a phallus on a monumental stone near the west gate of Carrawburgh, but — sorry, ladies — it's gone. A mole tells me it was taken away to adorn a home in the south of England.

The good news is that it's back. The bad news is that it's now kept in the dark in store at Newcastle University's Museum of Antiquities.

My mole, who can see in the dark, says it is "spectacular in size, girth and artistry!!!"

Carrawburgh is still worth a stop, however, to see the Mithraic temple.

Places to visit

Here's a selection of major sites — look out for others. The information here was correct at the time of going to press, but opening times and other details may change.

South Shields Fort (Arbeia): Baring Street, Lawe Top, South Shields, tel 0191 456 1369. Remains of a third-century depot which served Wall forts plus a reconstructed west gate. Excavations and re-enactments. Open Easter-September 30, Monday-Saturday 10am-5.30pm, Sunday 1pm-5pm; October-Easter Monday-Saturday 10am-4pm (closed Sundays). Closed Good Friday, December 24-26 and January 1.

Segedunum Roman Fort and Museum: Opening in Wallsend in June 2000. Tel 0191 295 5757. Includes reconstructions of military bath house and the Wall, with viewing tower.

Museum Of Antiquities, Newcastle (Pons Aelius): On the university campus, near Haymarket. Tel 0191 222 7846/7849. Roman and other collections. A model of Hadrian's Wall and a Mithraic temple. Open 10am-5pm daily. Closed Sundays, Good Friday, December 24-26, January 1.

Heddon-on-the-Wall: Fine stretch of Wall east of village, with circular medieval kiln. Open any time, free.

Corbridge Roman Site and Museum (Coria or Corstopitum): Half a mile north-west of town. Tel 01434 632349. Site of a succession of forts, a military depot and town based on what was the main road from York to Scotland. Museum objects include the Corbridge Lion. Open daily April 1-September 30 10am-6pm, October 10am-5pm, November 1-March 31 Wednesday-Sunday 10am-4pm. Closed December 24-26, January 1.

Brunton Turret: Just north of the village of Wall on A6079. One of the best preserved turrets. Open any time, free.

Chesters Roman Fort and Museum (Cilurnum): On Military Road (B6318) three-quarters of a mile west of Chollerford. Tel 01434 681379. Extensively excavated cavalry fort built astride the Wall and beside the Tyne. Roman bath house. Museum houses John Clayton's collection of altars, sculptures and inscriptions. Bridge abutment nearby. Open daily April 1-September 30 9.30am-6pm, October 10am-5pm, November 1-March 31 10am-4pm. Closed December 24-26, January 1.

Carrawburgh (Brocolitia): On Military Road (B6318) four miles west of Chollerford. Remains of fort built astride vallum, with late third-century temple to Mithras, the popular god from Persia. Open any time.

Housesteads (Vercovicium): On the Military Road (B6318) three miles east of Once Brewed. Tel 01434 344363. Claims to be the most complete Roman fort in Britain, with granaries, barracks, hospital and a famous loo (alas, not in working order) in a spectacular setting. Open April 1-September 30 10am-6pm, October 10am-5pm, November 1-March 31 10am-4pm. Closed December 24-26, January 1.

Vindolanda Fort and Museum (Chesterholm): Off the Military Road (B6318) One-and-a-half miles south-east from Once Brewed. Tel 01434 344277. Remains of eight forts and civilian settlements. Excavations going on. Reconstructions of Wall in turf and stone, Roman shop, temple and house. Museum has rare Roman writing tablets, leathers, textiles and pottery and wooden objects. Open daily February 13-November 14. February and November 10am-4pm, March and October 10am-5pm, later in April-September. Closed December and January.

Roman Army Museum (Carvoran): Off the Military Road (B6318) Three-quarters of a mile from Greenhead. Tel 016977 47485. The lowdown on life in the legions, how the Romans fought their way to the top — and more. Open daily February 13-November 14.

February and November 10am-4pm, March and October 10am-5pm, later in April-September. Closed December and January.

Birdoswald Roman Fort and Residential Centre (Banna): Incorrectly named on older maps as Camboglanna. On the road between Banks and Kiln Hill, Gilsland, in a splendid location one-and-a-quarter miles west of Gilsland. Tel 016977 47602. The fort was the site of a major excavation in the 1990s which showed occupation by the natives after the Romans had gone. Interactive visitor centre and fine stretch of wall and nearby milecastle. Open March 1-November 30 daily 10am-5.30pm (reduced hours in November).

Banks East Turret and Pike Hill Signal Tower: Four miles north-east of Brampton. Well-preserved turret and an earlier signal tower incorporated into the Wall.

Tullie House Museum, Carlisle (Luguvalium): Castle Street. Tel 01228 534781. Award-winning museum with interactive displays about Hadrian's Wall and life in the major town on the Wall in Roman times. Open daily Monday-Saturday 10am-5pm, Sundays 12-5pm. Closed December 25.

Notes for nerds

HOW to be a Wall bore — learn the following by heart and impress your friend(s):

The amount of stone used in the Wall was a million cubic yards (oh, all right, about 770,000 cubic metres. Doesn't sound so good, though, does it?)

Author Hunter Davies, who was raised at one end of the Wall in Carlisle, once asked a local civil engineering firm to calculate the cost of a wall made in concrete — £80 million at 1974 prices.

Length of the Wall was 80 Roman miles, which is 75 statute miles (120km).

Height of the Wall is calculated at 15ft (4.5m), or 20ft (6m) including a possible parapet.

Width of the Wall was 10 Roman feet (9ft 9ins or 3m); or, where the Wall was made narrower, 8 Roman feet (7ft 9ins, 2.4m).

Height of the turf wall was 12ft (3.5m), and the width 20ft (6m).

The defensive ditch was 27ft (8.2m) wide and 9ft (2.75m) deep.

Total width of the whole vallum structure was 120ft (36.5m). The vallum ditch was 20ft (6m) wide at the top, but only 8ft wide (2.5m) at the bottom. It was 10ft (3m) deep.

Highest-standing bit of Wall is just east of Sycamore Gap, where there's a bit more than 11ft high.

Highest point above sea level, 1,230ft (345m), is reached at Winshields near Once Brewed.

One Roman mile equals 1,620 yards (1.48km); one Roman foot equals 11.7inches (29.7cm).

Keep all this to yourself. Nobody else wants to know. Told you.

** Footnote: You can't have a history book without footnotes and this is the only one, so make the most of it.*

Dwellers beside the River Tyne are known as Geordies.

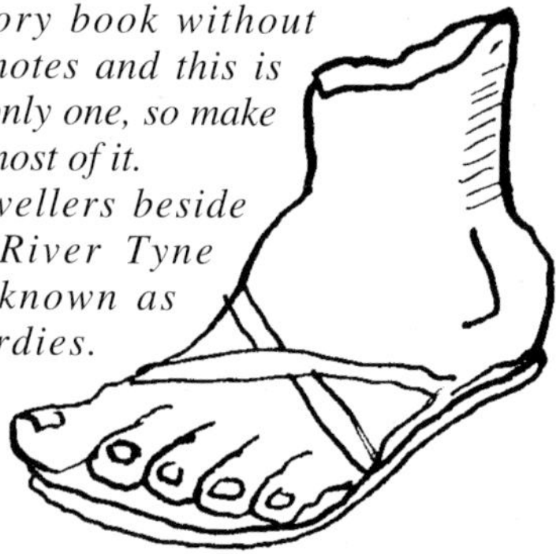

You knew that, but did you know that inhabitants of West Cumbria, at the other end of the wall, are known (at least to each other) as marras, a marra being a colleague or mate? A'-reet, marra?

That's yer lot, folks!

THAT'S enough. There's plenty more to say, but it can keep for another time.

The story of Hadrian's Wall keeps growing bit by bit as the archaeologists squelch around in muddy holes, leaving no stones unturned and brainily deducing all manner of things from dark and light patches in the soil.

Every year more bits of the jigsaw are put in place and there's plenty more alluringly bumpy bits of ground which have not yet been excavated.

Boggy ground has pickled for us centuries-old items made of leather, fabric and wood, including notes written on wooden tablets which give a glimpse of the individuals who lived along the Wall in its heyday.

Who knows what other finds are waiting to be made which will shine a light into the Wall's dark corners?

Enjoy your whizz along the Wall. Come back next year — there'll be more to tell.

Scroll on, readers!

AS WE say in the beginning, there are meatier books on Hadrian's Wall than this one.

If your appetite's whetted, English Heritage and the National Trust dish up longer guides. For even more facts (but fewer jokes) the weightier tomes and Ordnance Survey guide map listed here are recommended, but they're not the only volumes worth reading — look around the shops at the Roman sites, museums and information centres:

• Handbook To The Roman Wall, by J. Collingwood Bruce, 13th edition, revised, edited and enlarged by Charles Daniels, Harold Hill & Son, Newcastle Upon Tyne, 1978. ISBN 090046 332 5.

• Hadrian's Wall Historical Map And Guide, Ordnance Survey, 1989. ISBN 0 319 29018 2.

• The Northern Frontiers Of Roman Britain, by David J. Breeze, Batsford Academic And Educational Ltd, London, 1982. ISBN 0 7134 7256 1.

• Discovering Hadrian's Wall, by Dudley Green, John Donald Publishers Ltd, Edinburgh, 1992, ISBN 0 85976 365 X.

• Guide To The Central Sector Of Hadrian's Wall, by Robin Birley, Northern History Booklet No. 19, published by Frank Graham, Newcastle upon Tyne, 1972. SBN 902833 456.

• Life And Letters On The Roman Frontier, Vindolanda And Its People, by Alan K. Bowman, British Museum Press, 1994, ISBN 0-7141-1389 1.

• Roman Britain, by Malcolm Todd, Fontana Press, London, second edition 1997, ISBN 0 00 686363 9.